Leisure Arts 15

Painting
Portraits in Oils

Dennis Frost

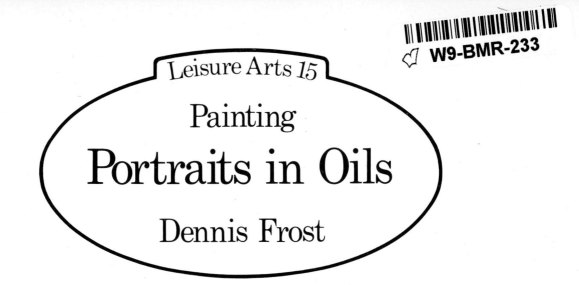

SEARCH PRESS LIMITED
London and Tunbridge Wells

TAPLINGER PUBLISHING CO., NEW YORK
A Pentalic Book

METHUEN AUSTRALIA

Introduction

Portrait painting is one of the most exacting subjects to tackle. Not only is the artist faced with the task of satisfying his own artistic judgement, but also the critical eye of the sitter, not to mention his close associates. Yet few subjects can give both painter and sitter such pleasure when the outcome is successful.

A landscape painter frequently has some latitude, and may, for the sake of good composition, 'move' a tree, or a building, to what he considers a more suitable site on the canvas.

A portrait painter has little such recourse except in posing the sitter, while even the removal of some disfigurement, may not be acceptable.

However, the painter is able to study the subject more sympathetically and subjectively than the camera, and with careful observation of features and mannerisms, he can produce a picture that is not only a good likeness, but gives insight into the sitter's character.

Requirements

Serious students of portraiture will avail themselves of the facilities provided by most local clubs and art colleges, which are able to offer skilled tuition, a workroom, models, easels, and quite often, painting materials. The classes usually consist of students of varying abilities, with a few star performers; my advice is to station yourself near to an experienced painter, note his palette, approach and the methods he uses to build up a picture. A class instructor also may be there to help and advise you, but I have found that the great value of these classes lies in studying the wide variety of techniques used by students to create their individual version of a subject.

Equipment

At times, however, you will want to paint away from the class. Although a well equipped studio is necessary for the professional, most students will need to compromise. Ideally the room in which you will be painting should have a good, constant, north light, your easel must be sturdy and able to withstand firm pressures without collapsing, and your palette, whether the traditional wooden type, or the paper, tear-off variety, adequate. Do invest in a selection of good quality hog-hair brushes, flat, filbert and round, and at least two smallish sable brushes for fine detail. You will need a jar of white spirit for cleaning your brushes, a jar containing an equal mix of linseed oil and pure turpentine for your painting medium, and plenty of clean rag.

There are a variety of supports, ranging from stretched canvases to commercially prepared painting boards, or even hardboard that has been sized and painted with an undercoat. The oil colours should be from a good quality Artists' range; bear in mind that the larger sized tubes are usually the best value in the long term.

Preparation for painting

Posing for a portrait can be tedious. Although the model should be prepared to sit for a stated time, frequent rest periods must be given. An interesting radio programme, or favourite taped music will often relax and entertain your sitter. When the model is a child, a visual stimulus, such as a bowl of goldfish, or a caged bird, will often hold his attention, leaving the artist free to concentrate on painting the picture.

My approach to portrait painting

When the preliminary negotiations regarding the number of sittings, the costume and the setting are completed, the first sitting can be started. During a sitting I like the conversation between us to flow for short periods; this way the sitter presents a variety of expressions without being aware of doing so, and one can observe how the shapes in the face alter, say, during animation and amusement, and so suggest not only the most appropriate physical picture to capture, but also the mood that motivated it.

Personally, I have an aversion to painting a broadly smiling or laughing portrait. It is all but impossible for the sitter to retain that sort of expression for the duration of a sitting and the strain involved is transmitted to me as the painter and the picture will suffer.

A smile completely alters the shape of a face. The eyes narrow, the cheeks widen and the distance between the top lip and nose shortens; humour, therefore, is not only conveyed by the shape of the mouth but also through muscular changes in the face and sometimes in the whole posture.

The preliminary sketch for the portrait is very important. If the shapes have been drawn accurately one can move on to colour and tone with confidence, but the drawing *must* be correct. To make sure, look at your picture through a hand mirror, for the reverse image will help to pinpoint any obvious faults.

Gallery

Portrait painting, to the observant painter, is as rich a subject-matter as any. On these two pages four heads are illustrated: ranging from *Girl in the Straw Hat*, (opposite) started and completed at a sitting of twenty minutes, through to the more finished portraits of *Young Girl with a Headscarf* and *Elderly Man with Beard*. From each of these I derived a different experience. Not only was my choice of colours different, but so was my whole approach to the way I tackled the depiction of my sitters.

With *Young Man in Profile* and *Girl with a Headscarf* I used a muted palette, warm brown tones being dominant. Notice how all the dusky skin-tones in the girl's portrait relate to the white highlight of the scarf on the upper temple. With the young man it was his hair and moustache that provided the salient characteristics of his head, offering interesting shapes not so apparent had I seated him full-face on.

The sketch of *Girl in the Straw Hat* represents how one might use the human head as a subject without faithful reference to actual physical features. It is not so much a portrait as a freely executed exercise in observing light and shade and the resultant colours on skin, textures and related background. Such studies, while not being strictly portraits, can liberate a tendency to paint too tightly and cautiously. Many students, when approaching portraiture for the first time, make the mistake of worrying and overworking the picture, the result then often turning out to be flat and uninteresting.

The vibrant expression of *Elderly Man with Beard* illustrates my point. With a freer technique and a more uninhibited palette with extra colours I felt I had succeeded in portraying the character of a notable local gentleman whose personality and vigour could best be captured by such an approach.

Portrait of a young man: demonstration

This is one of several paintings in which I used this young man as a model. I chose this demonstration to start with because of its cool colour range, thin paint and brevity of detail.

As a painter, one often feels a need to experiment with extremes of style. The usual pattern of progression in portraiture starts with a tight, photographic representation, and this is often followed by the desire to simplify the shapes and form to a minimum. There were many swings of the pendulum before I developed techniques that satisfied me and were acceptable to my clients. However experimentation is wasted, for there will always be new subjects that require a different approach.

Stage 1 (page 8)

Using raw umber I place the head and shoulders in an effective position on the board. The position of the features is indicated and a preliminary wash of raw umber worked into the hair.

Stage 2

The conversion of the line drawing into a tonal one is effected while the original paint is still wet. With a painting medium (half linseed oil and half pure turpentine) mixed with raw umber, some of the hard lines in the features are softened. Still working in raw umber, I paint in the hair and jumper, then rub over with a clean rag to achieve a flat tonal effect, eliminating the majority of the brushmarks. The rag is then rubbed lightly over the background.

Stage 3

The whole face is now reduced in tone, providing the foundation on which to build the tonal contrasts. Some of the darker areas are introduced into the hair and the jumper, and a thin wash of cobalt blue rubbed into the background. The paint is then allowed to dry before I proceed to the next stage.

Stage 4

When the paint has dried sufficiently to work on without lifting the underpainting, some colour is brushed into the face. Viridian and white are mixed for the shadows and a varying mix of alizarin crimson and cobalt blue used for the eyes. The flesh colours are achieved with cadmium red, yellow ochre, lemon yellow and white.

A little purple is placed in the background to echo the colour used in the face. The hair is darkened, and then the collar painted with flake white.

Stage 5 – the finished painting

Using a hog-hair filbert brush, and an absolute minimum of painting medium, the flesh colours are 'cooled' with a mixture of Naples yellow and terre verte. Cobalt blue, alizarin crimson and white produce the pearly greys used for the highlights around the eyes. The low key background is effected with Payne's grey and cerulean blue, and the collar overpainted with cerulean blue to reduce its intrusive whiteness.

Stage 1

Stage 2

Stage 3

Stage 4

Stage 5 – the finished painting

Drawing

Portrait painting not only implies an interest in physical appearances, but also in personality. I carry a pocket sketchbook with me almost wherever I go (a ringbound pad is ideal). As opportunities present themselves I make small sketches of poses, attitudes, expressions. Drawing is the vital underpinning for portrait work, whether a preliminary pencil sketch or when it is transmitted directly on the canvas with a brush.

Think of physical features as simple geometric shapes: cylinders, spheres, cones, planes – once these become apparent it is then easier to overlay individual characteristics. These pages show drawings which illustrate these points.

If it seems a little morbid to introduce a skull into a book about portrait painting, remember that it is the bony foundation for all portraits! Bones are the supports and anchors for muscles and the clothing of flesh that make up the human body. Studying anatomy cannot but help you in portrait and figure work. I draw as often as I can, studying shapes of heads, details of facial features, and postures. There is no substitute for practice.

Hands

Hands often form a vital complement to a portrait head. The hands on this page are in various attitudes of tension and relaxation and were drawn very quickly. My own left hand is often my model – and it can be reversed to a right hand if it is viewed through a mirror which inverts the image laterally.

Painting Features

On the following two pages (12–13) are oil sketches of features: eyes, mouths, hands, noses etc. Not only do such exercises make one familiar with anatomy but they help one to understand tonal and textural differences.

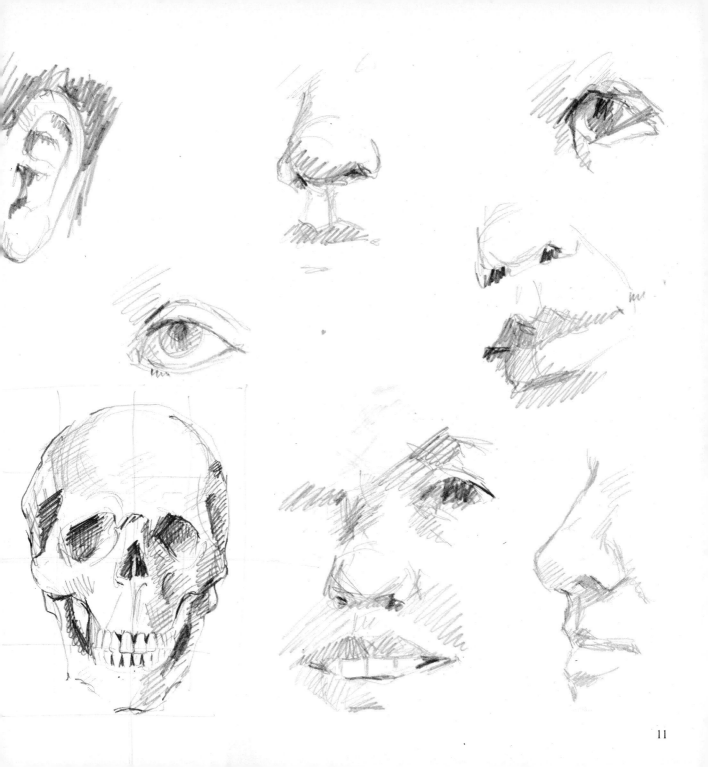

11

The Necklace: demonstration

One of the pleasures of painting elderly people is that their personality and character show more clearly in their features.

What once were smooth contours have weathered from without and within through a lifetime of experience: happiness, sorrow, pain, illness, contentment – all can be read from the face, hands, and posture of the elderly. In this portrait the posture and the hands are as eloquent as the face itself.

Stage 1 (page 16)

The drawing was made with burnt umber mixed with turpentine and linseed oil in equal proportions, using a No. 2 hog-bristle brush. A more diluted wash of the same colour was applied to cover the background and this was then rubbed over with a rag to give the board a flat covering which removed the original dominating white surface. This background colour will prove helpful when relating the tonal values (the darks and lights) in the early stages of the portrait.

Stage 2

With a No. 5 hog-bristle brush, the flesh tones are now blocked in, using cadmium red, yellow ochre and flake white. The features are sketched in lightly with alizarin crimson, flake white and cobalt blue. I will keep the paint well diluted when I mix cobalt blue and yellow ochre to produce the green of the cardigan. A mixture of cobalt blue and ivory black is used for both the dress and the lower background.

Although at this stage the painting appears to be a shadowy impression, it is in fact the foundation for the whole picture in terms of colour and tone.

The picture is then allowed to dry before the next stage is started.

Stage 1   *Stage 2*   *Stage 3*

Stage 3

The paint is now thickly applied and the picture begins to take on a more solid form with the strengthening of colour and tone throughout the whole subject.

To echo the colours used in the figure, a combination of lemon yellow, cobalt blue, cerulean blue and white are used to paint the background.

The features are then defined, using alizarin crimson for the warm areas and cerulean blue and white for the cool areas.

Stage 4 – the finished painting (opposite)

Practically the whole of the picture has now been re-painted, giving it a more solid form.

The features are worked in. In the elderly person there are marked colour changes throughout the face, the areas around the eyes and nose are warm and the flesh will appear uneven and colourful, as opposed to the smooth and even flesh tints of youth.

The hands are painted so as to emphasise the fact that they are large, bony and arthritic. Some of the edges around the head and figure are softened to merge them into the background. This helps to give a feeling of recession and avoids the aspect of a cut-out figure.

After the addition of cadmium red and white to complement the flesh tones, the background is subdued in order to give dominance to the figure. Finally the necklace is painted in.

Stage 4 – the finished painting

David:
demonstration

Child portraiture will require all of your patience, and a different type of setting-up from that explained under **Preparation for painting** (page 3).

You must be prepared for a child to be still only for very short periods, and you must mentally note the particular expression that appeals to you, and build up your painting of it each time it reappears.

Photographs can be a valuable aid when used in conjunction with the many sketches that precede an oil painting. You must also decide which style of work is most suitable for the sitter. I believe that an impressionistic style is not the most suitable for the very young: a simpler approach can capture the bright eye and smooth unlined skin to greater effect.

Stage 1 (page 20)

With a No. 2 hog-hair brush and using raw umber diluted with painting medium, the head and shoulders are drawn in and a thin wash of the same colour is introduced to state where some of the shadows will be.

Stage 2

More diluted raw umber is added to reinforce the tonal balance. The hair is blocked in and a little more tone applied to the face.

A diluted solution of terre verte is brushed into the background and then rubbed over with a clean rag, to give a flat area of colour which will complement the child's flesh tones.

Stage 3

The colours used to make the flesh tints are now added: yellow ochre, cadmium red and flake white. Burnt umber is used for the shadows in the face and cobalt blue and Payne's grey for the eyes. A little alizarin crimson is painted on the eyelids, and the shadows in the hair are deepened with raw umber.

Stage 4

At this stage the face is given greater detail. The shapes of the features are picked out in more definite terms and highlights added.

In order for me to achieve the effect I am seeking, a constant *paint and revise* technique seems the most successful route, and from an early stage in the painting all parts must go forward together, no areas being finally completed whilst others are still in a preliminary stage.

Stage 5 – the finished painting

For the final painting of the flesh, a very little medium is mixed into the colours, and terre verte and flake white made a complementary background for this young subject. The wistful, detached expression so noticeable in childhood is achieved by making the eyes regard a point over my right shoulder.

Stage 1

Stage 2

Stage 3

Stage 4

Stage 5 – the finished painting

The Feather Boa: demonstration

The opportunity to paint a portrait in costume is quite rare, and is all the more welcome when it does present itself, for costume gives the artist a chance to explore new and unusual textures. This actress had access to a theatre wardrobe and we tried several different costumes before deciding on the hat and feather boa.

Stage 1 (page 24)

The drawing is made with a No. 2 filbert hog-hair brush, using burnt umber. At this stage, although the shapes are drawn in sketchily, they are nevertheless reasonably accurate and the composition is set within the boundaries of the board. Any slight mistakes can be corrected as the painting progresses to a more solid form with the introduction of shadows.

Stage 2

At this stage I confine the tonal areas to the shadows on the face and hair, and under the hat. Raw umber is applied with a brush, and then rubbed over with a rag to give a flat tonal quality free from brush strokes. The areas to be painted in bright colours are left unworked.

Stage 3

Still using raw umber, the tonal values are built up on the face and hair before the introduction of other colours. Lemon yellow and cobalt blue are used in the background and the feathers blocked in using cadmium red, with alizarin crimson to give depth.

The paint is now allowed to harden before the work proceeds further.

Stage 4

The colours used for the flesh tones are yellow ochre, cadmium red and flake white. The dark areas in the features are suggested with a little burnt umber and cobalt blue. Cobalt blue is used for the iris and Payne's grey for the pupils. At this stage the face begins to take on more form, not only because of the light and dark passages, but also because of the introduction of colour.

Apart from colour enhancing the form, one must always bear in mind that it will influence, and be influenced by the costume colours.

Stage 5 – the finished painting

The features by now are extensively modelled, with particular attention having been paid to the eyes. The general tone of the flesh colours is lowered, in order that it be compatible with the shaded areas on the underside of the hat. The colour in the background is reduced in order to give more drama to the costume, and then the painting is left to dry again.

Once it is dry, I am then able to overpaint the feathers where they break into the background.

Some of the feathers on the hat are extra-downy and require a different approach; for this I use a sable brush.

Stage 1

Stage 2

Stage 3

Stage 4

Stage 5 – the finished painting

Len, a countryman: demonstration

Although this portrait was painted in my studio, I tried to achieve the impression of the outdoors, for Len is a groundsman at my local racecourse, and he spends most of his life out in the open.

Several preliminary drawings were made, from which I selected what I felt to be the most suitable position. Quick, thumbnail sketches can be invaluable in capturing the sitter's characteristics, without unnecessary details.

Stage 1 (page 28)

With my usual painting medium of an equal mix of pure turpentine and linseed oil, and using a No. 2 hog-hair filbert, I draw in the shape of the sitter lightly with raw umber, only a little attention being paid to detail.

Setting the subject in the most effective position on the board, with the proportions approximately correct, is very important at this early stage.

Stage 2

Using a light wash of raw umber, I convert the basic shapes into a tonal sketch. Once the outline or map of

the subject is stated, I start to think in terms of solid form and this blocking-in of lights and darks gives the picture the beginnings of a third dimension.

Stage 3

From the simple tone painting I progress to colour, keeping the painting very loose and working all the sections simultaneously. The flesh tones are made up from yellow ochre, cadmium red and flake white. Yellow ochre and cobalt blue are used for the green of the waistcoat. Payne's grey and raw umber are brushed into the coat.

Stage 4

At this point it is necessary to get more detail into the features. Some of the problems encountered when trying to suggest prominence or recession can be overcome by the introduction of lights and darks.

Beautiful shades of purple can be achieved by mixing together alizarin crimson, cobalt blue and flake white. By varying the proportions of these colours you can produce a range of warm, cool or pale hues. I use a very warm mix to shape the shadows under the nose and lips and a predominantly blue mix for the shadows under the chin and hat.

To complete this stage, cerulean blue, lemon yellow and white are applied to the background.

Stage 5 – the finished painting

Most of the extremes of light and dark, and the more extravagant colours are now modified as I work towards the completion of the portrait.

The old working coat and hat are darkened and kept free of detail which in turn help to emphasise the warm, sunny lights on the face.

Stage 1

Stage 2

Stage 3

Stage 4

Stage 5 – the finished painting

Using Photographs

I am sometimes required to paint a portrait using a photograph as the only source. Photographs can be an extremely useful aid to the portrait painter providing they are used for information and guidance, rather than being slavishly copied; for any painting, be it landscape, still life, or portrait, should reflect the artist's own skill and interpretation.

I rarely use photographs when the model is available, other than to record the setting and costume details, which can be painted without the presence of the sitter. Nevertheless a photograph is an acceptable basis for painting a smiling face; also when I attend functions that attract large numbers of people – markets, fairs, or race meetings – I always take my camera with me. There are so many interesting faces to be seen which will provide a rich source of inspiration for future paintings.

Most of my photographs are not taken in colour. This is not a matter of economics, but from choice, for I find that the limited amount of information provided in a black and white photograph encourages much more freedom of interpretation.

Other aids

Over the years I have built up a comprehensive library of cuttings from newspapers and magazines which provide me with further visual aids to possible poses and expressions. I have also drawn a series of outline poses which are pinned up on my studio wall. All these references I consult beforehand to help me decide how to position a prospective sitter.

But the best aid of all is constant practice – both at drawing and at painting.

ACKNOWLEDGEMENTS

Text, drawings and paintings by Dennis Frost

Text, illustrations, arrangement and typography
copyright © Search Press Limited 1982

First published in Great Britain in 1982 by Search
Press Limited, Wellwood, North Farm Road,
Tunbridge Wells, Kent, TN2 3DR

First published in the United States in 1982 by
Taplinger Publishing Co. Inc., New York, New York

First published in Australia in 1982 by Methuen
Australia Pty. Ltd., 44 Waterloo Road, North Ryde,
NSW 2113

National Library of Australia
Cataloguing-in-Publication data

Frost, Dennis, 1925–1982.
   Painting portraits in oils.
   Simultaneously published: London: Search Press.
   1. Portrait painting – Technique.   I. Title.
   (Series: Leisure arts ; 15).
751.45'42

UK ISBN 0 85532 458 9
US ISBN 0 8008 6421 2
Aust ISBN 0 454 00475 3

Made and printed in Italy by L.E.G.O., Vicenza